PLANTS ARE LIKE KIDS

Indoor and outdoor gardening

By JERRY BAKER
AMERICA'S MASTER GARDENER

Illustrations by **ROBERT PIERCE**

GROSSET & DUNLAP / PUBLISHERS
A FILMWAYS COMPANY

NEW YORK

CONTENTS

CONTENTS *(continued)*

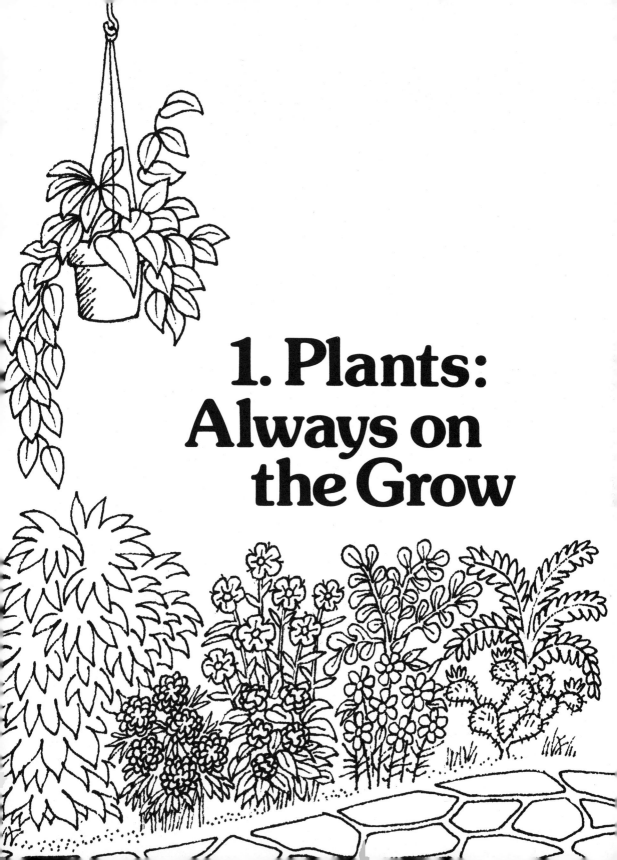

1. Plants: Always on the Grow

Which Way Do We Grow?

You have heard adults talk about having a "green thumb" when they talk about gardening, lawns, or house plants, haven't you?

Some folks say they have a "black thumb," which is supposed to mean that nothing will grow for them, while so and so has a green thumb and all he has to do is drop a seed on the ground, forget about it, and it grows like crazy.

The color of your thumb has nothing to do with growing healthy, happy gardens or plants. I am called a Master Gardener, and I don't have a green thumb. I ripened all over. I haven't been taught magic tricks or secret formulas. I was taught only to practice the four P's if I wanted things to grow for me. *Pride* was the first P I was taught. That means being proud of what you are doing and working hard to do it right. The second P seems to give most folks difficulty, and that's *Patience,* a must if you want to succeed. Patience is planning before rushing into something and then waiting for things to happen that you can't do anything about. The next P isn't exactly easy either, and that's *Persistence,* sticking with a job once you start it, even when it gets hard. You see, all of us were born with green thumbs and all we have to do to develop it, make it work, is *Practice.* That's the fourth P.

Why should you even bother to grow a garden, plant a tree, learn to take care of a lawn, or have a plant or two in your room. From what you see it looks like a lot of work. It is, but then anything worth doing is worth the work it takes to do it.

If you want to make the football team, school band, or cheerleaders, you work hard before you even perform for your classmates, but it sure is worth it when you hear the first applause. Well, growing things pays off in almost the same way. When you get a call from a neighbor who asks you to cut his lawn because you did such a good job for your dad, and he is willing to pay you, that beats any hand clapping I ever heard. Or, when a girl friend spends the night for a slumber party and asks how you get a sweet-potato vine to grow so long, that's recognition. Winning a ribbon for the biggest pumpkin at the 4-H fair, or selling your fruit, flowers, and vegetables for money at a roadside stand are both good reasons for learning how to grow plants. These are just a few good reasons. The best one may be hard to understand right now. It won't be long before you look back and say "Wow, am I glad I learned how to plant and care for growing things," when you have your own home and family and need to grow food for your table, or plants to make your home a pleasant place for your children to grow and learn in.

What should you grow? That's not hard to answer. I will do it with another question. What do you want to grow? I'll answer that question for you or we will be here forever, asking questions and growing older. You can grow anything you want to, indoors or out. Food, trees, or flowers, it doesn't make a bit of difference. The only thing you must remember is that when you invite a plant of any kind to grow in your house, you must make him or her happy. To do that you must make the place where your plant friend is going to grow seem as much like its real home as you can. Remember, plants were born in all different places in the world, like people, and they've moved around like people. We must learn what they like before we invite them to our homes because we may not be able to satisfy their basic needs, such as heat, light, water, food, and soil.

Not everyone has room for a garden and some apartments don't have big windows for growing plants. Money isn't always available for seed and plant food. None of these is a good reason for not joining the growing movement to become a plant person. There is a plant for every person and a person for every plant. All you have to do is learn the rules and your "green thumb" will ripen, not rot.

Plants Never Quit

"If I can't play third base and bat in the clean-up spot, I'm not going to play." "If I can't be the mother, I'm taking my dolls home." Have you ever heard a friend say something like that? Humans can learn a lesson from plants. They never quit, even when we plant them in the wrong place or forget about them. They just try harder. Many well-meaning people have planted vegetable gardens, brought home green plants, sown grass seed, planted rose bushes, put in shade trees, or started terrariums, then watered for a few days or a week or two, only to be disappointed. Weeds appeared as fast as carrots. The ends of the leaves turned brown on the green plants. There were more bare spots than grass spots on the lawn. Green leaves on the rose bush turned yellow. All the leaves fell off the new shade tree. It's enough to make some people quit, but not a winner. He remembers that plants are living things that from time to time have problems, looks for the cause, finds the cure, and earns the respect of his plant friend as a real teammate, someone the plant can count on. I think of plants as having human traits. From the looks of some folks' gardens and plants, it's a shame plants don't also have human actions so they could take better care of themselves. If you start a growing project, see it through to its conclusion. Be like your plants. Don't be a quitter.

Plants Have to Depend on You

I don't know of any person who likes to be taken for granted. Plants don't either. They need and want recognition. They want their own location, their share of food, and your attention. Plants, big or little, want to know you care what happens to them. When you see that something is wrong with them, you take care of it right then. Don't wait till a simple problem becomes critical. If you start a plant collection on a window sill, build a terrarium, plant a vegetable garden, decide to care for your neighbors' lawns and shrubs to earn spending money, or grow a flower garden for cut flowers to sell, you must learn to follow what we call a maintenance schedule. Every professional gardener does. It's a reminder list of what has to be done and when. Then stick to it. Just remember your plants' lives depend on it.

You and Your Plants Have a Lot in Common

I am always saying and writing that plants are like people, and it's true.

In order to stay healthy, we must get plenty of *fresh clean air, lots of sunshine, a balanced diet, soap to keep clean, water to quench our thirst, and proper rest.* Plants need exactly the same things for the same reasons. Plants cannot grow any better in a smoggy, dirty, polluted area than people or pets. Plants must breathe and they do this through their mouths, called stomata, derived from Greek. Most leaves have from 100 to 150,000 small mouths, which breathe in carbon dioxide and exhale oxygen. We need just the opposite, so we help each other. If soot or oil gets on the leaves they smother. If your nose and mouth became clogged, you would also smother. Next, plants must have sunshine to manufacture food. Called photosynthesis, the build-up of carbohydrates by chlorophyll-containing plants results in the healthy green color. If you place a green leaf in alcohol the green color will come out. Chlorophyll is a breath freshener for humans and animals. That's why parsley, to be eaten after your meal, is placed on your food plates at restaurants. If we get proper sunlight our tissues stay a healthy shade. If not, we become pale. Plants react the same way.

We all know what happens if we go without food, eat too much of the wrong food, or don't get proper vitamins and minerals. We starve to death or suffer from malnutrition, anemia, and so on. Plants are no different. To have healthy plants, we must make sure they get a balanced diet on a regular basis and, when they must spend months on end indoors, away from the sunlight, give them minerals. I water plants with a child's chewable vitamin with iron dissolved in the water. I take vitamins in the winter for the same reason.

I don't have to go into great detail about why we use soap and water on ourselves; but to make a comparison I will just mention a few reasons. First, to remove dirt from skin tissue so that the pores can breathe—same for plants. Next, to destroy fungus bacteria that cause skin diseases. You guessed it: plants get skin diseases like mildew. If you are a camper you know soap dislodges ticks, chiggers, and lice. Right on! Bugs don't like the taste of soap even on your plants so away they go. Always remember a clean plant is a happy one. That goes for fruit, vegetables, flowers, grass, and trees—all growing things.

Every living thing must wet its whistle (drink water) from time to time, and your plant friends are no exception. Some need more than others but they all need some. Here the thing to remember is to make it clean and fresh, with no salt. If it tastes good to you it will taste good to your plants. There is just one difference. Plants don't like cold water. Room temperature is best. By the way, your doctor will tell you the same goes for you. Cold water can give both of you cramps.

Plenty of rest for your plants may seem sort of far-fetched to most of you, but let's stop and do a little people-plant comparing here too. Without sleep your body would look like the dickens and in a short while you would stop growing. That's right, plants, people, and pets grow only in the dark, when they are at rest. Most plants need between eight to eleven hours of sleep. Just think about it; when does the sun come up and go down in June. Use the same schedule for artificial light in the winter. All you have to remember is if it's not good for you, it's not good for your plants. One last comparison: both plants and people began as seeds.

Light the Way for Your Plant Friends

You remember I told you earlier that light is necessary only for the manufacture of food and the maintenance of color of foliage and flower. Lights left on too long would stunt the growth of your growing friends. If you doubt this and have the heart to torture a plant, take two plants of the same kind, shape, and size. Care for both with proper food, water, heat, and cleanliness, but don't let one sleep. Keep the lights on day and night. In about ten days you will see the result. Now, to prove that plants grow in the dark, take another plant and keep it in the dark day and night, but feed and care for it properly. Otherwise it should be so tall, pale, and skinny in ten days, you can name it Stretch. By the way, if they left the lights on all night at a baseball field for weeks on end, they wouldn't have to mow it as often.

Sunlight is still the best light for man, plant, or pet, but if it's not available, any soft, white light bulb will do. The light needs to be just strong enough so that you could read without eyestrain if you were sitting where the plant is.

SAND   CLAY   PEAT MOSS

Your Plant Friends Need Firm Footing

Probably the most misunderstood part of gardening and growing is soil. You will notice I said *soil*, not *dirt*. No plant person would be caught with his trowel in dirt, only soil. The dictionary refers to soil as firm earth or the loose surface material of the earth in which plants grow, while dirt is referred to as a filthy or soiled substance. The so-called secret to a good growing surface was given away in the first few words, "loose surface material." This refers to sand, but water runs through sand, and plants would dry out. We must add something to the sand to hold the water a little longer so the plants get a proper drink, and that can only mean clay. Here again we have a problem. When clay and sand are together and the clay begins to dry we can get crusting. We can solve this with a flexible substance called peat moss, decayed plant material that is soft, porous, and nourishing to plants because it is organic. What, then, is a good all-purpose mixture of soil to insure firm footing for your indoor and outdoor plant friends? Equal parts of each: sand, clay, and peat moss.

Your Plants Would Like to See the Menu Before They Order

This part of gardening is sure food for thought. So that's what I am going to serve you, some simple common-sense thoughts. Back in the years before Christ, farmers fed their animals well so they produced good meat, milk, and manure. Farmers said that without plenty of the latter they would not get much of the other two because no grain would grow. When Columbus discovered the new continent, trees were large and nuts and berries were thick, but there were not many cows. So how did the plants live here? The leaves that fell and the needles that dropped, the grass that withered and the flowers that faded each year decayed and turned into the basic things green plants need:

Nitrogen: the element plants need for growing strong stems and green foliage.

Phosphorous: accounts for healthy flowers, fruit, nuts, and seed production.

Potassium: keeps plants from getting sick easily and promotes strong healthy roots for gathering of water and supporting the plants.

Magnesium, Manganese, and **Calcium:** the other things needed on the plants' dinner plate that were also found in the decayed humus, as it was called.

Like human beings, plants needed the so-called minimum daily requirements of trace elements—as it says on the sides of cereal boxes—in addition to the big six. *SULFUR, ZINC, BORON, COBALT, COPPER* and *IRON* make up the rest of the meal.

Today, as before Christ and after Columbus, leaves still fall, needles drop, grass clippings are cut, garbage is collected. We really should have no problem with lack of plant food, but we do because we are too lazy to carry it to the garden or build a compost pile.

When it is available, add fresh or dried animal manure—cow, sheep, chicken, dog, cat, turkey, rabbit, and others—to the garden patch in the fall of the year. On top of this, add leaves and grass clippings, then sprinkle garden gypsum (land plaster), one of Benjamin Franklin's

NITROGEN

MANGANES

PHOSPHOROUS

POTASSIUM

CALCIUM

MAGNESIUM

favorites, over this, spade it in, and let it set for the winter. Next season you will be known as the garden king in your neighborhood.

If you cannot get these materials, then apply any inexpensive "garden food" in liberal quantities in the fall.

Indoor green and flowering plants also need a regular diet. If you don't wish to waste valuable natural food, grind up your table scraps—but no meat or bones—in your blender with water. Strain off the pulp and store the fluid until you have a gallon. To this add 1 teaspoon of epsom salts (magnesium) and 1/2 teaspoon of household ammonia (nitrogen). Add 4 tablespoons of this to each quart of watering water along with 3 drops of liquid dish soap, and watch your house plant smile.

I might suggest that you use unstrained liquid compost (ground up table scraps) in your garden each evening without adding the ammonia and epsom salts.

I firmly believe that seeing is believing. Try this experiment with three pairs of plants—three foliage, three flowering—and feed one of each pair with liquid commercial, dry commercial, and one of each with Columbus Cocktail, as directed. If you do not wish to go to this trouble to see, then use a liquid plant food at 10 percent of the recommended rate in your watering water, along with the 3 drops of liquid dish soap per quart on house plants.

Bug Off

This is a hip phrase that came from the garden, which means "get away." So you see, we do have more in common with the plant kingdom than we think. There is another point to be made here when comparing plants and people. Insects cause plants pain and discomfort. Yes, Virginia, plants do have the same senses as humans. They have the sense of smell. They can die from gases, both natural and chemical. They have the sense of touch, like the mimosa plant (sensitivity plant), whose leaves fold up when it touches man or animal. They sense light, like the prayer plant, which curls its leaves up at night. They have the sense of taste, like the Venus fly trap, cobra plant, and pitcher plant, which eat insects.

Now, let's talk a little about pain. We know that plants are made up of cells. When you move cells and they run into other cells, they make noise (atomic cells). Scientists have recorded this sound. We will for the time being, then, until proven wrong, consider this pain. Now for our comparison: body lice, ticks, mosquitoes, chiggers, and chinch bugs burrow, bite, and suck fluids from our bodies and it causes pain and discomfort. Plant lice, borers, aphids, and worms burrow, bite, and suck fluids from plants, causing the same pain and discomfort.

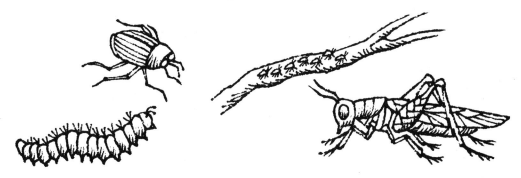

The first thing we do is take a bath in soap and water to rid ourselves of these pests and relieve the pain. Do the same with your plant friends. Wash them with Mom's liquid dish soap, using 1 teaspoon to the quart, or 1 ounce to the gallon outdoors. Plants that are inside should be washed every three weeks with a soap spray from your little sprayer. Outside plants should be washed every two weeks with a compression sprayer.

This is a preventive step as well as a minor cure. Insecticides (plant medicines) are used only when prescribed by an expert (someone called in at the last minute to share the blame) and then only in the strength and frequency directed.

All Plants Can't Swim

Aquatic plants grow in lakes, ponds, oceans, and rivers, not to mention aquariums. These plants swim and can't be overwatered. Both fresh- and salt-water plants can be purchased in a pet store, dime store, or aquarium shop. Plants like water lilies, which grow in both fresh and salt water, can be purchased at garden shops.

Cacti (cactus) are watered when the soil is bone dry; and succulents (cactus without thorns) are watered when the foliage is soft to the touch (easy squeeze).

Flowering and green plants are watered when the soil is dry to your touch. Let the water run all the way through. Here you must remember to add 3 drops of liquid dish soap per quart of water and 10 percent of the recommended plant food as well. Boy plants get boy food and girls get girl food.

For the purpose of identification, plants that have flowers or fruit are girls and require more phosphorus and potassium than nitrogen. Boy plants are those with heavy foliage, and they need more nitrogen. Refer to the plant menu section.

The liquid dish soap is added to improve penetration of the soil, as it is a soil softener. It also dislodges and discourages insects. Always be sure the water is at room temperature.

Outdoor watering is just as important as indoor watering. Lawns are always watered before 2:00 P.M. in the afternoon, preferably between 7:00 A.M. and 11:00 A.M.

The vegetable garden is best watered with a soaker hose from 11:00 A.M. to 2:00 P.M., and flower beds from 9:00 A.M. to 11:00 A.M. Remember, never let your garden or lawn go to bed wet.

Rain is food from nature, and I don't fool with Mother Nature.

Clay, or heavy, soil does not need to be watered as long, just more often, because the water runs away, not down. Sand, or loose soil needs to be watered longer but not as often; it runs too far down!

The best kind of sprinkler is free rain. Second best is one that covers a large area at one time and makes noise so I know it's working as hard as I am.

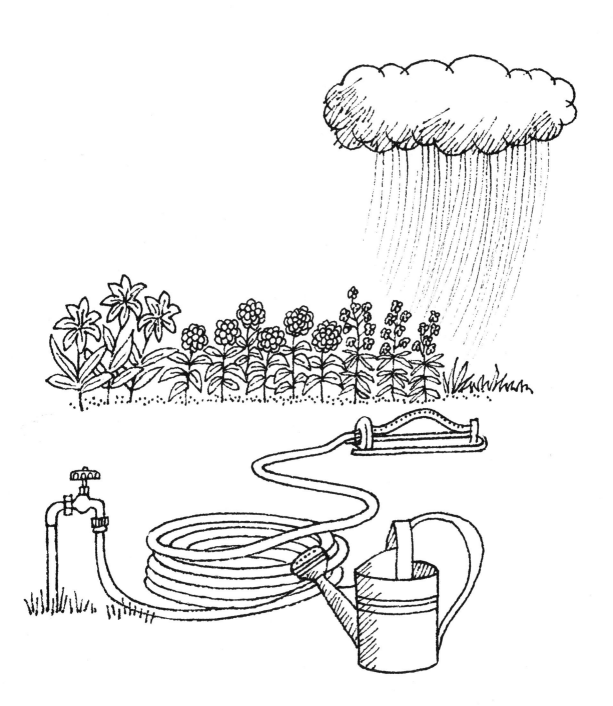

Plants for All Seasons

We seem to forget that man as well as birds, animals, and plants all lived in the Garden of Eden together without the benefit of a house. The trees and flowers were as much a part of our way of life as the rest in the garden. Why not bring them back into our lives? The more plants you have in your home, the better your health will be, especially in the cold areas of the world. You will have fewer colds, your breathing will be better, and your temper may improve. How can a few plants do all of this? You will recall that I stated earlier that in order for a plant to be happy and grow, you would have to duplicate its normal living conditions. Most plants, when growing indoors, like a day temperature of 72 degrees and a night temperature of 68 degrees, while the humidity (moisture) should be 40 to 50 percent. That happens to be the recommended comfort zone for humans. As a rule, we keep our homes too hot and dry. This is why we catch cold when we go out during the winter months. This is also why plants won't live long in our homes in the winter. If you will try the 72-68 degree, 45 percent formula, both you and your plants will stay healthy and happy. Now, with a proper comfort zone you can plan ahead and have tulips, hyacinths, crocuses, and daffodils inside in bloom from January to March, lilies from March to April, mums and azaleas all winter. Not to mention any one of 13,000 green and colored foliage plants from a few inches tall to as high as your ceiling.

It's Timing That Counts

The old saying about being in the right place at the right time is a commandment to a plant person. If you want a colorful array of flowers, thick green grass, juicy fruit, and tasty vegetables, you must *plant ahead.* Use your imagination to see the colors that will appear in the spring when you are planting tulips, hyacinths, and crocuses on a cold, gray November day, or sowing early seeds like lettuce and radishes when the soil is still cold in April. Every seed packet, perennial box, or bag of bulbs has a colorful picture to stimulate your imagination. This is done on purpose by the marketing people. On the same bag, box, or packet is an introduction to your plant friend with instructions on when, where, and how to plant and care for him or her and planting them on time.

Don't Call a Doctor for Cuttings

All plants do not have to be started from seed. You can start some by taking a piece from an older plant, which is called a parent plant, and rooting it in a pot by itself to grow into a mature plant. This saves both money and time. These are called cuttings. There are softwood cuttings, such as geraniums, coleus, impatiens, dogwood, wandering Jew, and ivy. The others are called hardwood cuttings, and they are honeysuckle, poplar, privet hedge, and wisteria, to name a few.

Softwood cuttings are 3- to 4-inch-long soft growths taken from mature plants in early May and June. Cut them with a sharp knife and dip the stem about 1 to 1 1/2 inches into a special hormone called Rootone, which stimulates quick root growth. Fill a large wood or metal container that has good drainage with sharp sand (builder's sand) and soak it down. Next poke holes in the sand, about 2 inches deep and 2 inches apart, and place the dipped stems into them, making sure not to rub off the hormone powder. Keep new cuttings damp, but not soggy, in a shaded spot where the temperature is maintained at about 70 to 75 degrees until growth begins. Then dig up the seedlings and place each in its own pair of shoes. Three inch clay pots are good-sized baby-plant shoes. Why do I call pots shoes? Plants' roots are their feet, soil their socks, so the pots are the shoes. Do not transplant a new cutting to a larger shoe until its feet (roots) grow through the hole in the bottom, and use a shoe that is only one size larger.

Take *hardwood cuttings* in late fall when the leaves have fallen. Tie several 8 inch long cuttings together and store them in a box of sawdust or peat moss in a cool cellar until after the frost has passed. Dip the stems in at least 2 inches of Rootone and then place them 3 inches deep into the soil where you want them to grow. Keep a close eye on these baby plants.

Almost any rooting-hormone package will give you a full list of both hardwood and softwood cuttings.

Never start a new plant in a glass of water and then move it to soil. Nine out of ten times it will die because the pressure of the soil and richness of the food is too great for it.

Don't Shiver Their Timbers

Climate and temperatures are the most important things in your plants' lives. Pay close attention to your local weatherman and your newspaper. Never take indoor plants outside for the summer until you are sure there is no chance of frost. Do not plant small seeds in the ground *until* you are sure the soil temperature is above 45 degrees. Use an ordinary outside thermometer to be sure. If frost is forecast, cover young vegetable and flower plants with milk cartons, hot caps, or boat hats made from newspaper and do not remove them before 10 A.M. The trunks of newly planted fruit and shade trees should be wrapped with a tar paper, and young evergreens and flower shrubs covered with burlap material, while roses are covered with leaves and soil 10 to 12 inches high. Spread twigs over the tops of perennials and bulbs and cover them with straw. I always put snow suits and boots on all my garden friends, to insure their health and comfort, when the weather calls for it.

Indoors you must move plants at least 12 inches from a pane of glass and away from outside doors, where cold drafts will strike them. If the ends of the leaves turn black, the plant has been frozen. Remember what I said earlier about you and your plants and temperatures of 68 degrees at night and 72 degrees during the day? Keep a small thermometer near your plants.

Cold air is not the only discomfort to affect your plants, indoors and out. Warm, dry air can hurt your plants and the ends of the leaves will turn brown. You can find a draft by lighting a candle and placing it where the plant is. The flame will indicate the direction of the draft.

Outside, you must protect your trees and shrubs from the southwest in the winter and the west in the summer. If you are ever lost in the woods, look for large trees that have a long split up and down them on one side. The split will always be on the southwest side of the tree because in winter bark thaws out on sunny days except in the shaded areas and continues to swell until it splits. In the summer the drying wind is always out of the west. Young or soft plants must be protected by a larger, stronger plant or a wall. Vegetable gardens should always be protected on the west by corn or sunflower plants.

House plants should be placed on the northeast to east side of the house, out of doors. Those that stay in the house all summer (shame!) should be kept out of direct sunlight through glass panes , which tends to cook them, like their cousins the vegetables. A sheer curtain is also a great help. You only have to remember that if you are uncomfortable in a certain location, so are most plants.

2. Gardening: Who's Who

Know Your Fruits From Your Vegetables

From the following list pick out the names of five fruits: potatoes, asparagus, carrots, peppers, apples, peaches, tomatoes, cucumbers, cabbages, and beets. That's right, half of the plants named are fruits. In addition to the obvious apples and peaches, you may have guessed tomatoes, but now the going gets tough. Here I will give you a hint. A *fruit* is an ovary, the part of a flower in which seeds are produced. You've got it: pepper and cucumber.

Now, can't you just see your mom saying, "For dessert tonight we are going to have fruit salad," and then serving a mixed salad of peppers, squash, cucumbers, and so on.

The word *vegetable,* on the other hand, is the term used for herbaceous plants (plants that do not have woody tissue) that grow from seed and die at the end of one growing season, with the exception of asparagus and rhubarb, which live year after year.

To take the confusion out of which was fruit and which vegetable, gourmet's decided that any plant eaten during the main course was a vegetable, and during dessert, a fruit. Just to confuse things further, at gourmet restaurants in Europe they still serve salad after the main course.

With that bit of trivia behind us, let's get into why you should plant vegetables and where, when, and how.

Why should I plant a garden? I could say for the fun of it, and on the other hand I might suggest it would keep you healthy, both in body and mind, and keep you from getting bored. Then again I might just suggest that you could make money. So, to answer your question, all of the above reasons are why you should plant a garden. Gardening can be fun if you use your head and plan before you plant, so that it doesn't take a lot of your playtime. There has never been a question that when you are out in the bright sun and fresh air you look and feel better. As for the mind bit, after you play hide and seek with a tomato hornworm (a big green worm), and he wins the game and eats a few of your tomatoes just when they were getting ready to go to market, you will turn on the old brain power to win the next round. Now, how could you possibly make any money by planting a garden? Simple! Every wife buys vegetables at the store, but women prefer fresh grown better. Plant fast-growing popular vegetables and later sell them from door to door, or put a stand up on the corner as you did when you sold lemonade when you were smaller. I know many young men and women who helped pay for some of their education this way or earned extra spending money. And, by the way, they lived in the city.

Where do I find enough room for a garden? Let's begin at home. Ask your dad if you can have a 10 by 20 foot patch and the unused space along any fence. You will also do him a favor and make a bare spot under a tree, where no grass grows, look pretty good. You might tell your dad that you can get him out of having to paint the rain gutter downspouts for another year, and promise your mom that the edges of the front walk and driveway will be the talk of the neighborhood. Next, many churches, banks, towns, and cities have community garden patches or vacant lots that you may get permission to use.

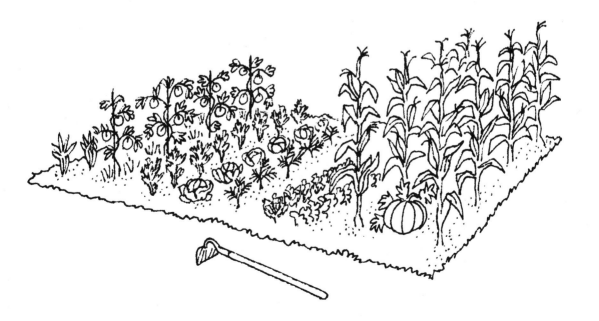

When should you begin your garden project? As soon as you have made up your mind that this is a project for you. The best time to prepare the soil for a garden is in the fall. Next best is the early spring, when the soil will crumble in your hand. In either case, you add the same stuff. First, you must select your location, get permission, decide on the size, draw up a plan or layout to scale on a large sheet of paper. I use a shopping bag, opened up, and draw my plan with colored felt-tipped pens. Select the kinds of vegetables you think will sell best. A trip to the supermarket with your mom will help. Look at the produce counter. This will give you ideas.

The first year stay away from fancy foods and stick to summer squash, acorn squash, straight-eight cucumbers, Honey Rock melons, Bell Boy peppers, Dark-Red Detroit beets, Cherry Belle radishes, Bonnie Best or Marglobe tomatoes. Your dad may have a suggestion or two as well. In almost every magazine that comes to your home, there are offers for free seed catalogs. Send for them early in the winter so that you can order your seeds and have them on hand. Some seeds can go directly into the ground as soon as you can work soil with your hands and it won't stick together. The frost must be out of the ground. You can check this by placing a regular thermometer into the soil and making sure the temperature is above 45 degrees.

How do you go about preparing the soil, plant feeding, and keeping the bugs away? The first thing is to pick the proper location, and that's in full sun, level ground, and light soil. Now you can begin to prepare. You must remove all wood, glass, metal, large stones, and other debris. Next, spread grass clippings, leaves, or peat moss, 5 bushels of each—any or some if they are available—for each 100 square feet of garden, that is, 10 feet long and 10 feet wide. On top of this, 25 pounds of lawn and garden gypsum, 10 pounds of garden lime, and 10 pounds of any garden food. You now spade this under to a depth of 8 to 10 inches with a hand spade or a roto tiller, which means you may need Dad's help, both physical and financial. The garden surface must be as smooth and level as though you were going to plant grass seed. Refer to your plan, making sure you know which direction is north. Now begin to plant. Corn is always on the west; pumpkins among the corn. Spinach, lettuce, and greens are next; while potatoes come after that, with garlic and onions planted among the potatoes for protection against bugs. Carrots, radishes, parsnips, turnips, and beets can go one after the other. Then comes cabbage, with tomatoes as neighbors. Cucumbers, squash, and melons are always last, and plant them on the east end, as they are always on the move and grow toward the morning sun as a rule. Always leave room enough between the rows so that you can get your big feet in to work when the plants are babies.

If you have planted your garden from seeds, then you must wait until they are an inch or so high before you can lay down *mulch* (a soil covering), grass clippings, straw, sheets of newspaper, roofing paper, or black plastic. Build up grass and straw to about 4 to 5 inches as the plants grow. Lay down three sheets of newspaper and then cover with 1 inch of grass clippings. Roofing paper and plastic need not be covered. Mulch keeps you from having to hoe, weed, or water as much and saves a lot of hard work. Watering is done generally from noon to two P.M., about three times a week. Feed your plants every three weeks. Melons, squash, the cabbage family, leaf plants like spinach, and lettuce are fed lightly by sprinkling grass fertilizer on the soil or mulch between the rows. Beets, carrots, tomatoes, radishes, and all other root vegetables are fed the same way with a garden food that is lower in nitrogen.

If you look at any bag, box, or bottle of fertilizer or plant food you will see a combination of three numbers, plainly visible. For example, a common lawn-food fertilizer is 10-6-4, while a garden food will consist of 4-12-4. A house-plant food for green plants (liquid or dry) might read 7-5-8, while a blooming house-plant food might easily be 6-10-4.

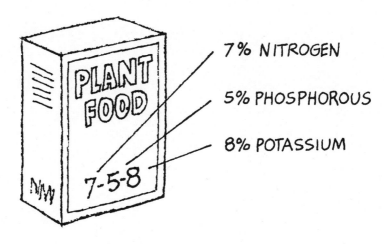

7% NITROGEN

5% PHOSPHOROUS

8% POTASSIUM

PLANT FOOD

7-5-8

What these numbers mean and what some folks think they mean are two different things. Some folks think these are the odds on whether the plants are going to live or die. In some cases the way people use fertilizer that's what it works out to be. The real meaning is that the first number always tells you how much nitrogen (for leaf and stem growth) is in that box, bag, or bottle in proportion to the total weight of that container. The next number is always the amount of phosphorous (the flower, seed, and fruit grower)—again this is a percentage of the contents—and the third number is the potassium content (the health food and root developer).

You remember that earlier I referred to girl plants and boy plants? Well, as you progress in school you will learn in biology about sexual propagation of plants with seeds and spores, and asexual propagation of plants, using the foliage, stems, buds, and other vegetative parts. But for now and for the purposes of making you understand how to feed plants I am going to tell you how my green-thumb teacher explained the difference. *Girl plants* are plants that grow (produce) flowers, fruit, or vegetables. *Boy plants* are all leaves and greens. Many of your science teachers will say this is too simple an explanation and I agree, but I don't have the time or space to go into it now.

Tooling Along

We have seen movies where the hero was trapped underground and all he had in his possession was his mess kit, which had a knife, fork, and spoon. The only real way out was to dig, so that's what our hero did, but the hard way—with a spoon. Ten years later, with a long white beard, our hero reached the surface only to find that someone had built a skyscraper over him. The moral of this story is: be prepared. When you go exploring, carry the tools of the trade. Our hero should have had a pick and shovel.

The same goes for the growing explorers. You cannot afford to own all of the tools made for gardening and plant growing, nor do you need all of them, but you do need the basic tools of the trade. A hoe, rake, and shovel are needed for outdoor growing and a fork and spoon for indoors. There is not much to remember, only that tools should always be clean and sharp when you begin a garden job and cleaned and sharpened when you finish. The easiest way to pass a disease from one plant friend to another is with dirty tools. It's just like eating with someone else's silverware before it has been washed when he is sick. When you finish a garden chore, wash the soil off your tools with the hose, wipe them dry with a rag, and rub on any type of oil (auto, home, or food) to prevent rust. Sharpen the edges of hoes and shovels with a number-10 file (ask Dad to use his). If you have been working around a sick plant, wash the tools with Mom's dish soap, dry, rub alcohol, and then oil. This is to kill the disease or insect causing the problem. Just remember any tool you use must be clean and sharp.

Indoors is the same except the tools. You thought I was fooling when I said a spoon and fork, didn't you? I am serious. The small indoor tools that are available are great for looks and do a good job, but an old dinner fork with the tines bent over 1/2 inch makes a rake, and an old tablespoon and teaspoon bent up on the edges with pliers make two different shovels. You can also cut a 1 foot long piece of wire coat hanger and bend a finger ring in one end for aerating (hole poking), and you will have the proper tools for the trade.

Seedlings Run Faster Than Seeds

Your garden can be started from seeds sown (planted) right into the ground, which cost a lot less, about 1 cent each, but take longer to get vegetables. Or you can buy what we call seedlings, or bedding plants, from the garden center or greenhouse. These are seeds that were sprouted in a greenhouse early in the winter and transplanted (moved) into larger pots or boxes (flats or trays) to grow stronger and larger, so you can plant them outside in your garden when frost is past and get vegetables faster. The cost for each plant bought this way is from 6 to 8 cents each. Then again, you can start your seeds indoors just as the man in the greenhouse does.

My Mom Won't Let a Greenhouse
Sleep on Our Couch

That's a silly title for the subject of growing seeds indoors, but some folks really think you need a big greenhouse to do this job right and that it takes a lot of money and time. They are wrong on both counts. It is nice to have a greenhouse and maybe someday you will be able to join "the glass-house gang" and have your very own greenhouse. For now you can have a small portable one that you can ask for, for a birthday, Christmas, or Arbor Day (a joke to tell your folks). What you want to ask for is a GRO-VARIUM. It's a miniature greenhouse that sits on a table or bench in the basement or your room, which keeps the soil at 74 degrees because it has a built-in thermostat. I call it an electric blanket for seeds. It also has a tall plastic dome with small holes to control the moisture (humidity) and air temperature. This means perfect growing temperatures, top and bottom, so you can grow plants faster and easier.

Let's get started. Before you plant any seeds, whether it be in the ground or in your little greenhouse, place them in an ordinary cup of tea, green, orange, or black, makes no difference. Then place the cup in your refrigerator (not the freezer) and leave them there for four days.

At the end of the four days remove them, drain off the tea, and spread the seeds out so that they will dry enough to handle. Now you may plant. Why? Why what? Why do you put seeds in tea and then into a refrigerator? I thought you would never ask. To fool the seeds into thinking they have just slept all winter just as they would have if they had been growing wild. You see, the tannic acid in tea stimulates (wakes up) seeds quicker, while the low temperature in your refrigerator, 38 degrees, puts them to sleep. When the temperature goes below 40 degrees all plants go to sleep (become dormant). When you take the seed out and they wake up they do not know whether they were asleep for two hours, two weeks, or two months. They just know that they must start growing. Try that one on your folks and they will think you know some magic when they see the results.

The best mix to start new seeds indoors is a material called sphagnum moss, which looks like seaweed (your dad uses it in his bait box to keep worms healthy). We use this because it does not let disease that can kill new baby seeds get started. Get the moss wet with warm water containing 3 drops of Mom's liquid soap per quart. Then squeeze out all the extra water and fill the tray of your Gro-Varium or a metal or plastic cake pan loosely. Now you may sprinkle the seeds on the loose bed of moss, or drop them about 1/2 inch apart so it will be easier to move them to their own shoes (pots) a little later. Cover the little seeds with a thin layer of damp moss, maybe 1/16 of an inch. Fill an empty window-sprayer bottle with weak tea, then spray mist, making the moss damp, not soggy wet. Cover with Gro-Varium lid or a layer of plastic food wrap, and place it in a dark, warm spot. The Gro-Varium has its own built-in heat. If you use a pan, place it on or near a heat register.

The new baby seeds should sprout within a day to a day and a half. When you can really see the new plants, about two or three days later, move them into regular light, but not bright sunlight. You may now lift off the cover, but keep the heat in the tray at 74 degrees. Keep the moss barely damp with the spray mist, but not soggy. After four or five more days you may make the temperature a little cooler, 65 degrees day and night. (See how you treat baby seeds like baby brothers and sisters?) If they are kept too warm they will grow very tall, weak, and skinny, and fall over. Watch your baby plants closely and when they have two sets of leaves, it is time to move each one to his own shoe (pot), or plant both in a community flat of wood.

First things first. I use only clay pots for work shoes, 2 1/4 inch clay pots that have been soaked in warm water until they stop bubbling. Fill the pots with a mix of equal parts of sharp sand (builder's sand), garden soil, and damp sphagnum moss. Now, with your little finger poke a hole in the soil in the middle of each pot. Next, gently remove each baby plant from the tray, using a table fork. Any moss that clings to the roots may be left on. Set them down at least halfway up to the stem and

into the hole you have poked and gently firm the soil around them. Spray mist and place them in a cool, 65 degree, well-lighted area, and care for them as you would regular boy or girl house plants until the threat of frost has passed. Then plant them in your garden.

I have made a list of how early, how often, and how late you may plant your vegetable seeds in areas where the winter temperatures get below 40 degrees and it snows. The southern and western areas of the country have an extended season or more than one growing season. Consult your Grandpa and Grandma about their arthritis. If it hurts, don't plant. If it doesn't, go ahead and plant. Flower seeds known as annuals (plants that live their full life cycle in one season, like vegetables) are planted in April in cool parts of the country, in January in warm areas. Seeds for cut flowers are started the same way as vegetable seeds.

All Bulbs Don't Light

Flowers that grow from bulbs, such as tulips, crocuses, daffodils, hyacinths, narcissi, and snow drops, are known as fall plants and are planted at that time. These bulbs (fleshy subterranean buds) are planted after the first frost to make sure they do not wake up before it is time. In warm parts of the country, you may plant bulbs in January or February. In Florida and Southern California it is a good idea to pre-cool bulbs (store in the refrigerator for five to seven weeks) and then plant. Do not use the tea secret on bulbs.

Bulbs can be forced to bloom indoors all winter, as long as they are pre-cooled in the refrigerator or in pots buried in the frozen ground for ten weeks, brought into a warm, dark place until they begin to grow, and then moved to a bright 65 to 70 degree room, to fill the house with Mother Nature's perfume during the gray, cold days of winter. This is a great surprise gift for parents, grandparents, or good friends. A super project for you guys.

Don't Laugh at a Pansy

You have heard or will hear an old dumb phrase as you grow along, referring to a man or boy who may not be as large boned or dress as most people think men should. He is referred to as a "pansy." That's a stupid comparison to begin with, since a pansy is one of the toughest plants in the garden. People are, of course, saying he is a sissy or he acts like a girl. Joe Namath was in an advertisement wearing women's panty hose, and I dare anyone to call him a "pansy."

The pansy and her sisters are called biennials. They live two or three years, unlike their cousins the annuals, which live only one year. The biennials are planted in the fall of the year from seed and produce foliage the first spring and flowers the second and third! They are seldom started in greenhouses, but are sown directly into the soil. Biennials are an excellent buy for the money because you get three times the life. Other biennials are hollyhocks, English daisies, forget-me-nots, foxgloves, Canterbury bells, and sweet Williams.

You Can Count on Some Plants Forever

We would all like to live forever, but we just can't seem to find the secret. Plants have, but they, like people, have a tendency to be selfish and keep some secrets to themselves. The perennials are the biggest offenders. They are the flowering plants that live year after year and grow healthier and more beautiful as they grow older. They are also real producers. Perennials, the strongest of my flower friends, like cool weather and produce color in my garden long into the fall. You must, however, be careful about where you allow perennials to homestead in your garden, or they may soon run another growing friend right out of its home. Make sure you know all there is to know about the perennials

you invite to live at your home, so that you do not have to embarrass yourself and the perennial by asking it to move on. Plant perennials from seed (you can start them in the Gro-Varium) or wait until the frost has passed on and the soil temperature is 60 degrees or higher. Perennials may also be purchased as mature plants to be planted in full bloom in early summer or throughout the summer and early fall, like hardy chrysanthemums.

Perennials should be divided in the spring at three-year intervals. Dig up half the plant and move it to a new location or trade it to a friend for a plant you do not have. There are a lot of perennials to choose from. Here are a few of my favorites: bleeding heart, candytuft, chrysanthemum, columbine, day lily, iris, larkspur, painted daisy, Oriental poppy, peony, phlox, and primrose.

Corms Is Not a Misspelled Word

Like people, plants' feet have different shapes. You remember I said plants' roots are their feet. Well, feet that have different shapes have names, such as flatfeet, clubfeet, webfeet on ducks, and hoofs on horses, deer, and sheep. The same goes for plants. Corms describes crocus and the gladiolus feet, and they have a real problem. They work so hard every year that they wear themselves out and their new babies, called cormels, grow up on top of the foot (corm) like little lumps. I will bet that your folks and your teachers do not know that the sore lumps that grow on their own feet when their shoes don't fit were really called corms by our forefathers because they looked just like cormels. Someone should tell Dr. Scholl he misspelled corn plasters.

You Can't Play Music on a Tuber

But it sure is music to the ears of a farmer or a kid who likes to hear Dad ask if he wants some french fries. That's it, kids, the potato is a foot called a "tuber," and so is the begonia's foot a tuber. The tuber foot is the only plant foot that can see where it is growing because it has eyes. To grow more tubers you cut them up, but make sure that each piece has an eye so he can see where's up.

Rhizomes Are Not Space Stations

Though they act like space stations rhizomes like lily of the valley or common lawn grass are also plants' feet. The rhizome pushes itself out underground, extending little feelers that look like the legs on the lunar module that lands on the moon. They are called "pips," and new plants are grown from the baby feet called pips.

Sprouts Can Jar You

Along with this area of growing, I might add, don't be a "spoil sport," because I am going to keep you in the "dark," and I mean really. If you had a room with no light at all, pitch black, you could grow all of the food you would need for both nourishment and bulk and not have to use any more space than it takes for a record player. Now, how's that for a riddle?

The plants I have just described are sprouts and mushrooms. These plants grow in the dark, contain no chlorophyll, are fast to produce, contain large quantities of vitamins, and take very little work. Five to 6 tablespoons, which cost from 7 to 10 cents can provide you with enough of a balanced diet for a week. I am sure that at least a few of you are wondering who eats sprouts besides bugs. You do! When you eat chop suey or most other Chinese dishes. Your folks do when they order salad in most expensive restaurants (gourmet). Ask your mother to buy some canned or raw sprouts for you to try. How you eat them depends on what you like to eat. Let me give you an idea of which seeds you can sprout, and then I will make some suggestions for you to give to your mom to enrich her meals with proper nutrients. The most common seeds for sprouting are mung beans, alfalfa, wheat, rye, lentils, buckwheat, lettuce, radishes, soybeans, peas, clover, sesame, oats, and lima beans.

Sprouting seeds is easy and not expensive. I like plastic cottage-cheese or butter cartons. Other containers that may be used are fruit jars with pieces of cloth over the openings, pans, pots, and dishes, but the plastic cartons, one on top of the other, are the easiest and cheapest. They are called a Japanese Sprouting Garden. To sprout seeds in these containers, turn them upside down and poke twenty-four small holes in the bottoms of all except the one that will be on the very bottom (we will stack them one on top of the other). Next, cut a 2 inch square opening in all the lids except the one that will be on the very top carton. In this one poke twenty-four small holes with a small nail. In the bottom of each carton place a folded paper towel or napkin that has been dampened. You may now decide which seeds to sprout. I suggest you try mung beans and alfalfa, which Mom can buy in the grocery or health-food store.

Soak your seeds in a cup of weak tea overnight or for about eight hours, then place them on the damp paper towel in the cartons. The number of seeds you put in will sprout to about seven times the space of the small seeds—1 tablespoon of seeds become 7 tablespoons of sprouts. Put the lids on the cartons. The following day begin to water by pouring cold water into the top lid with the small holes. Use 1 cup of water each morning for each stack of 5 cartons for five days. At the end of five days take the sprouts out, wash them well with cool water, and eat them.

Mung beans can be used in vegetable dishes, tossed salads, cole slaw, and potato salad. *Alfalfa* can be used with fruit juices, salad, sandwiches, and soup. *Soybeans* can be used with scrambled eggs, malted milks, and salad.

Mushrooms are another source of food that can be grown in your home or outside. Small kits for growing mushrooms are available in the fall and winter from seed or mail-order houses and garden centers. Mushrooms are grown from spawn. The plant you eat is called *fungoid,* and its root is *mycellium.* You can purchase two types of spawn. Bottle spawn, produced in a laboratory, or manure spawn, produced in natural conditions. This is a fun project for winter months and a great science project. Mushrooms like night temperatures of 50 to 55 degrees and day temperatures of 70 to 75 degrees. They like damp rich soil that has lots of manure and leaves mixed into it. Never pick or eat mushrooms from outside unless you are with an adult who knows the good guys from the bad.

You Don't Need a Music Conductor to Lead You in the Hydroponics

The dictionary described hydroponics as "the growing of plants in nutrient solution." What that really means is growing plants in water with food added and no soil to keep them growing straight. Greenhouses that grow tomatoes hydroponically have large tubs in the ground with wire mesh over the top and wire or string to guide and to tie the plants. Hydroponic growing is good for desert areas, where water is hard to come by. If you would like to try hydroponic gardening, take two glasses, fill one with plain tap water and add a tea bag that has already been used to make two cups of tea. Next, add 4 drops of liquid plant food (if you are growing a girl plant use girl food; for a boy plant use boy food) and then put the stem or piece of plant into the water glass with at least two-thirds of the plant out of the water. Set the plant in a comfortable location with a good view. As the water evaporates (disappears) add more water, tea, and food. The plant will develop roots, grow, and flower. Fill another glass with cotton, tightly, and poke

a hole all the way to the bottom with a sharp nail. Put another stem into the hole, letting two-thirds extend above the edge, and add the same mixture, replenishing as it disappears. One plant is free standing, the other is root supported. You can also use marbles or rocks for support. That's hydroponics. Keep your eyes open to notice the difference in color of the leaves, flowers, or fruit, as well as the taste. Nothing beats soil grown for beauty and flavor.

House Pet Plants

The words "house plants" would lead you to think that only a few special plants can be grown inside your house. That is not true. Any plant that grows outside can grow indoors "if" you can make the inside of your house just like the plants' real home outside.

Before you invite a plant to come live with you, find out as much as you can about it: what kind of climate it likes, the heat and light it needs, and the food it eats. Some plants will take more of your time than others, while some others are loners. They just like to be left alone. They don't take up much of your time. You must find out how tall they grow and how fat, and above all how fast. It wouldn't do for a plant to move into your bedroom as a small baby and ten to twelve weeks later you have to move out because there is not enough room for both of you in the room. Your public or school library has many books on house plants, with special information on the likes and dislikes of many plants that might interest you. I have written two books on house plants called *Make Friends With Your House Plants* and *I Never Met a House Plant I Didn't Like.*

Rather than try to talk about the hundreds and hundreds of plants you could choose from—some expensive, some not—I am going to tell you about some easy, simple, overlooked plants that you can grow to decorate your room or to give as presents. You might also want to grow them to sell.

I will bet that you think I am going to give you the names of real fancy plants that come from deep in the jungles of South America, where most of the house plants we buy in plant and flower shops come from. Wrong. These plants grow deep in your own garden.

If you would like to have an upright growing plant with green leaves that your pet dog or cat won't bother, why don't you plant a summer-squash seed or zucchini-squash seed in a 6 inch clay pot filled with garden soil. Or, you may want vines to grow up the window, a stick plant, watermelon, cucumber, or cantaloupe. If you want leaves with lots of color, plant coleus seed, or impatiens for flowers. Carrots or parsnip seed can be grown as mock ferns, sweet potatoes for vines, and avocado pits for indoor trees.

Here's how to grow plants from seed. Remember I said to soak the seed in weak tea and refrigerate for a few days? Well, that's *step one*.

Step two is to soak the clay pots in clean warm water till the bubbles stop. *Step three*, fill the pots with good, rich garden soil. *Step four*, poke a hole in the center of the soil 1/2 inch deep. *Step five*, place the seed in the hole and cover it with soil. *Step six*, place a folded newspaper over the top of pot for three to five days or until the seed has sprouted. *Step seven*, when sprout is showing, move the plant into a well-lit room. *Step eight*, take 1 quart of rainwater, add 3 drops of your mom's liquid dish soap, and one tenth of what they say to use on your mom's plant-food box or bottle. Use this to water your plant when the soil feels dry to your touch. Do not water again until the soil feels dry.

If the plant is an upright plant like the squash, rotate the pot a half turn each day so it grows straight and fat, otherwise it will lean toward the light. If it's a vine, like cucumber, place it next to a window and don't move it. It will grow up and around. If you place one plant on each side you will have a living frame.

Plants talk in sign language, expressing themselves by the things they do. If the ends of the leaves turn black, your plant is freezing. If the ends turn brown, it is in a warm, dry draft. If the leaves drop from the bottom, you are over-watering and if they drop from the top, you're not watering enough. If the big leaves turn yellow, you are not feeding enough, and if they start to turn brown from the inside out, you are feeding too much. If the new leaves are yellow, the plant needs vitamins or a mineral like iron. Place your baby brother's or sister's vitamins on the soil.

Insects don't all stay outside and your plant can catch cold, have athlete's feet, measles, and acne. To keep your plants clean, wash the leaves every two weeks with a light soap and water bath sprayed from a spray bottle. To stop bugs, have Dad cut a pest strip into 1 inch squares and put a piece on the soil. That will take care of that and any flies in the house, as well.

The amount of light your plants need is the same as you do, twelve to fourteen hours of good reading light. In addition to the light from the window, 60 to 75 watt soft white light bulbs will do.

"Hey, You" Is Not a Name

All plants have a Latin botanical name. I flunked Latin, so I have to rely on the next name that all plants have. That's called a common name, like maple, oak, carrot, ivy, and so on. Now plant people go a step further and give their plants personal names. For instance, all African violets have personal names like Pink Lady, roses have names like Dinah Shore, peppers are called Bell Boy.

With a waterproof pen print the name you give your plant on the rim of the pot and draw a smiling face on the side under its name. Remember, girl plants get girl names and boy plants, boy's names. I have named all of the trees, shrubs, and evergreens in my garden, and they wear an identification bracelet so visitors will know who they are. Does the name make them grow better? You will have to decide that yourself. Seeing is believing.

Say a Kind Word

Talking to plants has been a well-discussed subject for some years now. I even wrote another book called *Talk to Your Plants*. Scientists have been experimenting with lie detectors on plants to see if they have feelings, and none seem to agree. As a small boy I was always taught that "plants are like people." The name of my first book was *I Lived With My Grandma "Putt,"* and she talked to her plants as she worked in her garden. When the petunias would grow over into the geraniums' part of the garden, she would scold them by saying, "Now girls, you have your own bedroom (because plants grow in beds). You stay out of your sisters', " and she would gently reach down and guide them back. Or she would compliment the rhubarb with a phrase like "You sure do look handsome, Frank, all decked out in your red pants and green head." Well, let me tell you, I was afraid that my grandma was going crazy the first time I heard the conversation, so I came right out and asked why she was talking to the plants and if they talked back.

She said, "Now, Junior (that's my nickname), everybody knows plants can't speak out loud. They make sign language (I explained that earlier), but I know they understand what I mean because they smile."

"How does a plant smile, Grandma?" I asked.

"By blooming or growing big, pretty, tasty food."

So kids, I talk to my plants and it works for me. Besides, Grandma Putt had one more word of wisdom. Moses talked to a burning bush and Christ to a fig tree, and who's going to doubt them.

They Don't All Like Rock Music

Do plants like music? The question has been pondered for years and scientists have come to the conclusion that plants do grow better with music than without, again not through any magic means, but because of a real thing. The real thing is really two, so it should be things. One is vibration (jiggling), and the second is moving currents (breezes).

If a plant just sits on your window sill or dish and gets watered the soil is packed down and it pinches the plant's feet (roots). Its arms (branches) get stiff because it is not doing the exercises it does when it is bending to and fro in the wind outside. If you put your plants on top of your radio or stereo and play music that has a heavy base beat (boom, boom, boom), it causes the plant to jiggle. This moves the soil or loosens it so that food and water can get to the roots. Sound, as your science teacher has or will teach you, moves air, which causes the foliage to move and gives the arms exercise. You can also brush your hand on the foliage (pat your plant on the back) and blow on your plant from time to time, which helps move or exercise the foliage. Place your

hand on top of the radio and see if you can't feel the bass beat, or tape a piece of thin tissue at the top in front of a speaker, turn up the sound, and watch the paper lift up. As I said before, seeing and feeling are believing.

A Good Neighbor Policy Can Insure a Perfect Vegetable Garden

Every one of us has a best friend or a group of friends—kids we have something in common with. Plants are the same, and some are better friends than others. This is called compatibility. It is a good idea to know which plants have something in common, such as the water, food, heat, or light they need. Following is a list of plants that like to grow together:

- Asparagus, parsley, and tomatoes
- Beans, corn, carrots, beets, cabbages, celery, and potatoes
- Beets, beans, onions, kohlrabi
- Broccoli, dill, cabbages, mint, sage, rosemary, cauliflower
- Carrots, lettuce, chives, onions
- Celery, beans, potatoes, cucumbers, cabbages
- Corn, potatoes, peas, beans, melons, pumpkins, cucumbers, squash
- Cucumbers, corn, cabbages, potatoes, radishes
- Fruit trees, garlic, nasturtiums, chives, onions, mustard
- Lettuce, carrots, radishes, strawberries
- Onions, beets, carrots
- Peas, carrots, cucumbers, radishes
- Potatoes, cabbages, corn, beans, marigolds, horseradishes
- Radishes, nasturtiums, peas, lettuce
- Roses, chives, onions, garlic, marigolds
- Spinach, strawberries, beans, lettuce
- Tomatoes, marigolds, parsley, cabbages, cucumbers, potatoes

You will notice that in some cases flowers and vegetables or flowers and trees make good neighbors, and you may wonder why. Insects pester certain plants but leave others alone because they don't like the taste or smell. These are called plant antagonists. You can protect a vulnerable plant by surrounding it with a plant that repels the bugs that attack it. This is the reason for growing some plants close to one another.

Your Garden Will Get a Charge Out of This

I am sure that in the last few years you have read about or heard your science teacher or parents talk about the need to harness our natural resources. Some of you may have wondered what they meant. A farmer puts a harness on horses so he can control them. They help him to do his job, plow a field or cut hay or cultivate corn, faster and easier. Man wants natural resources such as coal, iron, oil, timber, water, and copper to help him. He has found it and used it to his best advantage.

But some of these are becoming harder to find, so he must look for more sources of energy to help him. He looks at the sun, wind, and rain. But in most cases he overlooks a real helper. If our gardens, grass, and trees could talk out loud, they would give you the answer in a flash! They would say lightning. Now you are really confused. Right? What good can lightning do besides frighten the by-gollys out of us and make us hide under the bed covers? It makes food for our garden and growing friends by converting the atmosphere to pure nitrogen, the

growing friends by converting the atmosphere to pure nitrogen, the food all plants need. The grass, trees, and flowers are always brighter after a storm . . . and even we feel better. You can convert the atmosphere around your plants by attracting electrical charges, called static electricity, by using metal or nylon items to support or tie your plants. This is called electroculture by organic gardeners. It really works. Tomatoes, beans, and cucumbers should be staked with metal poles, not wood, and tied with pieces of old nylon stockings. Peas, bush beans, and lima beans should be grown on a wire fence or chicken wire. Stretch wire (copper wire is best) over row crops such as carrots, radishes, and spinach and let the plants grow around it. You may want to tie small pieces of nylon stockings a foot apart on the wire. Try some plants with metal and some with wood. Then notice the difference.

No One Has All the Answers

The older you get the more you will understand that you must always try to learn more. In this book I have told you only what I know. Some people won't agree with what I have said, or they will think I have made it too simple. That's good. They are entitled to their opinions. What I try and find to work is good for me. You may find a way for you that's even better. People who garden, work on their lawns, or grow plants are of different religions, colors, and nationalities, and they speak different languages, dress differently, and eat differently. Plants are the same. They come from foreign lands, like different foods, and are different colors. What all people and all plants have in common is they are all soil brothers and soil sisters.

3. Planting Guides

Plan for a Small Vegetable Garden

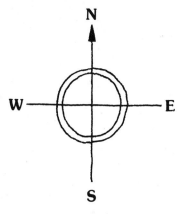

Here is a good plan for a small, 8 by 12 foot vegetable garden. Corn is planted on the west, with pumpkins between the rows. Tomatoes are supported with old metal stakes. Squash and cucumbers are supported with chicken wire. These vine crops are always planted at the east end of the garden. For more information on planting your seeds to get best results see page 60.

LIMA BEANS

PEPPERS (STAKED)

CORN 3 SEEDS PER MOUND

SPINACH

LETTUCE

12" APART

PUMPKINS (BETWEEN ROWS OF CORN)

ONIONS

12'

BUSH BEANS

PATH

RADISHES TURNIPS CABBAGES

SQUASH

8'

12" APART

18" APART

POTATOES

CARROTS PARSNIPS BEETS

CUCUMBERS

GARLIC
(BETWEEN POTATO PLANTS)

PEAS

TOMATOES

POLE BEANS

Vegetable Gardens

Here are some vital statistics for planting your vegetable garden: how deep and how far apart to plant the seeds to ensure their comfort, when to plant them, and how long it takes for them to mature.

Vegetables	Depth of Seeds	Distance Between Rows	When to Plant	Maturation
Bush beans	2 inches	3 feet	May, June, July	60 days
Lima beans	2	3	May, June, July	60
Pole beans	2	3	May, June, July	60
Beets	1	1	April, July	60
Broccoli	1/2	2	April	70
Brussels sprouts	1/2	2	April, July	90
Cabbages	1/2	2	April, June	50 to 100
Carrots	1/2	1	April, July	70
Cauliflower	1/2	2	May, July	45 to 70
Celery	1/2	6	May	110
Corn	2	2	May, June, July	70 to 100
Cucumbers	1	4	May, June, July	50 to 57
Eggplants	1/2	2	May	60
Garlic (bulbs)	1	2	April, May	90 to 110
Lettuce	1/2	1	April, May, June, July	45
Melons	1	4	June	60 to 90
Mustard greens	1/2	1	March, April, September	30 (root 50)
Onions	2	1	March, April, July	30
Parsnips	1/2	1	April	90 to 100
Peas	1	2	March, April, May, July	60 to 90
Peppers	1/2	2	May, June	60 to 75
Potatoes	3	3	April, May	60
Pumpkins	1	4	April	50 to 60
Radishes	1/2	1	April, May, late August	25
Spinach	1/2	1	April, August	45
Squash	1/2	1	May, June, August	50 to 100
Tomatoes	1/4	3	May, June	45 to 70
Turnips	1/2	1	April, August	50

Decorative Plants

Before planting your flower garden, decide what you want. Some plants grow well in the shade; others make colorful borders. There are plants that are just right for window boxes that add color to the outside of your home, while others are great for cut-flower bouquets. Check out the following charts, then plan your garden.

Tall Plants, 36 inches to 6 feet, suitable for backgrounds and cuttings	Amaranthus Aster Celosia *(giant)* Marigolds Zinnia *(giant)*	
Medium Height, 18 to 30 inches, for cuttings or borders	Balsam Carnation Celosia Dahlia Marigolds *(mosquito chaser)*	Nicotiana *(fragrant)* Petunias Salvia Snapdragon Zinnia
Plants for Cut Flowers	Asters Carnations Celosia Centaurea Cosmos Larkspur Marigolds	Nasturtiums *(bug chaser for fruit trees and bushes)* Salvia Snapdragon Verbena Zinnia
Plants for Window Boxes, Planters, and Tubs	Allyssum Coleus Lobelia Cascade petunias	
Low Plants, 6 to 12 inches, for borders	Ageratum Alyssum Begonia	Calendula Coleus Impatiens

Low Plants	Lobelia	Portulaca
(continued)	Marigold (dwarf)	Snapdragon (dwarf)
	Pansy	Verbena
	Phlox	Zinnia (dwarf)

Plants That Grow in Shady Areas	Balsam	Impatiens
	Begonia	Lobelia
	Browallia	Nicotiana
	Calendula	Salvia
	Coleus	

House Plants

Do you remember what I said you should do before inviting a plant to your home? That's right. Make sure you can provide the same conditions indoors that your plants are accustomed to outdoors. This chart tells you what each plant likes: the amount of light, water, humidity, heat, and the type of soil. Using the key below, follow the chart. Then watch your plants thrive.

Light: bright—B; medium—M; shade—S
Water: wet—W; damp—M; dry—D
Heat: normal (68 degrees)—N; cool (55 degrees)—C; warm (74 degrees)—W
Humidity: normal (40 percent)—N; dry (15 percent)—D; high (60 percent)—H
Soil: light (1 part soil, 2 parts peat, 1 part sand)—L
medium (2 parts soil, 1 part peat, 1 part sand)—M
heavy (3 parts soil, 1/2 part peat, 1 part sand)—H

Foliage Plants	Light	Water	Temperature	Humidity	Type of Soil
Aspidistra	M	M	N	N	M
Avocado	B	M	N	H	M
Cactus	B/M	D	N/W	N	L
Coleus	B	M	N	H	M

Foliage Plants	Light	Water	Temperature	Humidity	Type of Soil
Dracaena	M	M	N	N	M
Dumb Cane	M	M	W	N	M
Ferns	M/S	M	N	H	L
Ficus	M	M	N	N	M
Ivies	M	M	N	N	L
Norfolk Island Pine	M	M	C	H	M
Palms	M	M	W	N/H	M
Peperomia	M	M	N	N	L
Philodendron	B/M	M	N	N	M/H
Piggyback plant	B/M	M	N	N	M
Schefflera	M	M/W	N	N	M
Spider plant	M	M	N	H	M/H
Wandering Jew	M	M/W	N/W	H	M/H

Flowering Plants	Light	Water	Temperature	Humidity	Type of Soil
African violets	M	M	N	H	L
Begonia	M/S	M/W	N	H	H/M
Geraniums	B	M	C	H	M
Impatiens	B/M	M/W	N	N	L